Forging a Great Brand

The Brand Architecture Workshop
Leader's Guide with Worksheets

David A. Okrent

September 2015

Heart-Centric Marketing - Seattle, Washington

Forging a Great Brand
The Brand Architecture Workshop
Leader's Guide with Worksheets
By David A. Okrent

David A. Okrent
Okrent Consulting Services
Seattle, WA 98118
info@okrentconsultingservices.com

No part of this book may be reproduced or transmitted in any form or by any means, electronic, mechanical, including photocopying, recording, or by any information storage and retrieval system, whether for commercial or non-commercial use, without written permission from the author, except for the inclusion of brief quotations in a review or scholarly work.

The purpose of this workshop guide is to educate. The author shall have no liability or responsibility to any person or entity with respect to any loss or damage caused, or alleged to have been caused, directly or indirectly, by the information and opinions contained in this workshop guide. If you do not wish to be bound by the above, please return the guide as soon as possible.

ISBN-13: 978-0692514290 (Heart-Centric Marketing), ISBN-10: 0692514295

Copyright 2015 by David A. Okrent, all rights reserved worldwide

Every company is capable of having a fantastic high-earning brand, but few attain one, why?

Because most companies lack a straightforward tried and true process for converting the brand strategy, brand architecture, and brand personality into organizational and individual actions. This workbook and guide reveals a step-by-step approach to help businesses create a market-driven brand strategy, architecture, and personality, and shows them how to convert these items into actions that make the brand a positive force in the marketplace. Using this process a firm can develop and deliver a brand that customers will love and ideally competitors will fear. Imagine what a firm can do when it can deliver a fantastic brand experience consistently.

Why a fantastic brand? Because a fantastic brand helps companies achieve significant earnings over their competition and are more attractive to investors. This guide is for people like business consultants, marketers, brand managers, product managers, owners, CEOs, CMOs, entrepreneurs, or anyone that wants to create brand equity by becoming deeply meaningful and desired by potential customers.

This book is dedicated to Elizabeth - my wife and friend and my children Jacob and Sarai.

Table of Contents

Prologue 1

Know the Business - Know the Brand 5

A Few Notes from the Front Lines 8

Worksheet 1 – Business Environment 15

Worksheet 2 – SWOT Analysis 18

Worksheet 3 – Target Customer Segment 21

Worksheet 4A – Firm's Personality Defined 25

Worksheet 4B – Firm's Personality Described 28

Worksheet 5 – Courtship 32

Worksheet 6 – Differentiation 35

Worksheet 7 – Purpose 40

Worksheet 8 – Brand Architecture 45

Worksheet 9 – Attribute Narratives 51

Worksheet 10 – Brand Personality 57

Reversing the Process: Brand Personality to Opportunity Selection 59

Worksheet 11 – Positioning Statement 61

Another Sneak Peak at What's Next 64

Using the Worksheets 65

Prologue

Introduction

Every company, organization, and person has a brand – a reputation and/or something someone associates with the firm or individual. For example, the burger joint down the street, a friend, and even a passing stranger all have a brand, story, or reputation applied to them by those that see, hear, or think about them. These brands are constructed from direct and indirect experiences, feelings, cultural beliefs and values, related associations and memories, and assumptions and judgments of the beholder. This internal representation defines an individual's concept of something's or someone's brand or identity. Based on this brand the viewer makes choices.

During a lecture on brand, I once put up a series of three slides. The first slide contained the image of a famous male comedian and I asked the audience what they knew about this person. Then I put up a slide with a picture of a female singer and asked the same question. I then pointed out these are their individual brands. Next, I put up a slide with a picture of a stranger in a Belgium train station and asked the same question as before. People began to construct a story or brand for this person - someone they knew nothing about. We are constantly trying to make sense of our environment and to help us navigate through our worlds we tend to consciously and unconsciously "brand" the people, places, and things around us.

Although each person creates their own perception and meaning of a specific brand, the objective of the company or organization is to create a set of meaningful, relevant, and repeatable experiences to help set a common definition and expectation with the target market. Unfortunately, for many companies and organizations the process is often a mixture of unconscious and conscious intention rather than being a deliberate fully conscious act that is planned, resourced, and executed throughout the organization. This workbook supports those desiring to have a conscious intention on brand development and delivery.

The Logo is Not the Brand

Many companies focus their brand development primarily on creating a catchy name and graphic. However, the choice of name or graphic is not important, because these are only symbols for the brand and are not the brand itself. Names and logos only serve as memory cues to help the potential customer recall what they know about the firm and its offerings. Think of the pictures of the comedians mentioned earlier as logos, or memory cues, about their reputation. When these types of firms contact us for help in brand creation they are often surprised when they find themselves soon talking about their corporate culture, processes, and structures.

It is a bit of an exaggeration to imply there doesn't have to be a relationship between logo, name and brand. Ideally, the logo and name need to evoke the attributes of the brand. Thus, the brand definition and personality informs the design of the logo and name. Firms that get fixated on creating the perfect logo first may neglect what actually makes a fantastic brand.

What is a Brand?

Over a decade ago, I began focusing on brand development and management. During the early years of this work, I spent time learning, thinking, and experimenting on what creates a strong brand - one that would garner the highest value in the market.

Generally, one can define brand as the sum total of the market's collective impression of the firm and its offerings through direct and indirect knowledge and experiences. However, that doesn't directly indicate how to create a brand, let alone a great one. I was interested in the process of creating a fantastic brand.

What I eventually determined and confirmed is that brands are the products of behaviors - simply, "brands are behaved." Specifically, a firm must behave its way into the hearts and minds of its target market based on what is meaningful to the customer while being competitively differentiated from its competitors. This is in contrast to an often held belief that advertising creates the brand identity. Great brands behave their way to greatness first, then brag, and not the other way around.

Companies with strong brands generally have significantly integrated their unique brand behaviors into their organization and offerings. Then they use promotional Marketing and Communications (Public Relations) to help get the firm noticed and to set a behavioral expectation in the market. Customers experiencing the fulfillment of these expectations consistently over time will begin to see the brand favorably and prefer it over competitors. However, if the advertising message and the firm's behaviors are incongruent, that is, less than advertised, then the market will label the firm a weak brand. Firms that consistently disconnect in this way from their promoted expectations tend to have short lives.

This also means, the market bestows the label of strong or weak brand on a firm based on the firm's actions and behaviors. To put it another way, market/customer perceptions determine the firm's brand strength. The firm can't anoint itself a great brand - the market does.

Figuring out what these "brand behaviors" are and how to integrate them into the company or product led me to create the Brand Workshop Series. Over the course of a decade, these workshops have been refined based on the implementation of their results. There are five workshops in the series each one consisting of two to three-days of intensive work. This guide contains the worksheets used in *Workshop 1 – Brand Architecture*.

Pay-Off - A Strong Brand

The goal of the workshop process is to provide a firm with a blueprint for creating a strong memorable brand. If the firm is committed to converting the blueprint into reality it will reap benefits like a loyal customer base, easier access to capital, support for a higher offering price, attention by trade and other media, and higher employee retention and productivity rates.

You are the Target Market for the Guide

This workbook and guide is for business consultants, marketers, brand managers, product managers, owners, CEOs, CMOs, entrepreneurs, and anyone that wants to improve the success rate of their business endeavors. The information and worksheets in this guide will help firms build fantastic brands.

The guide portion of this book is not a comprehensive textbook on brand development and management. It is my notes and thoughts on the workshop, some commentary on branding, and a little preaching from the pulpit thrown in. I provide some background to support each worksheet and to give you a view into what went into its design. Profits and non-profit organizations will find this guide and its worksheets equally helpful on defining their brands.

The Core is Enclosed

Missing from this document are the exercises, participant training materials (for example, what is a brand and why it affects the bottom line), and other worksheets that provide input to the ones enclosed. However, in each block on the worksheets there are sufficient questions to help guide the user in completing the sheet. Many of these blocks or questions may be broken out as separate worksheets and exercises if desired. There is a description section before each worksheet where I touch on some of the additional activities I use during a workshop. The items I omitted from the guide do not take away from this guide; these parts only reflect my facilitation and training style. Removing these items made the guide more efficient for others to use.

Of course, these sheets don't provide the answer; they are only a vehicle to help arrive at the definition of the company's or organization's brand.

It Takes a Group

It is best to do the worksheets in a group consisting of different levels of management, members of all departments, key non-managers, and people of different ages and backgrounds. Keep the numbers to less than twenty-five. In cases where the firm is a start-up or relatively small it is still best to do the work in a group, bring in friends and others to help.

Shameless Plug

Here is a list of the workshops we offer:

Workshop 1 – Brand Architecture

Workshop 2 – The Brand Implementation Plan

Workshop 3 – Brand Personality and Expression

Workshop 4 – Managing for Brand

Workshop 5 – Customer Loyalty by Design

Strategic Planning Seminar

Integrated MARCOM Planning Workshop

Business Therapy Weekend

We also offer other business services including product and business development support.

Know the Business - Know the Brand

The brand is the behaviors of the firm through its people, processes and offerings. If a brand is only the behaviors of the firm then just selecting some attributes like good customer service, quality, competitive price, have fun, wear red, act like a hipster, and be exciting might be all it takes to begin attracting customers and money. This can work (see "Reversing the Process" later in the guide), but I don't think it's as effective at maximizing success as following this process, which starts by focusing on the business fundamentals.

My method starts with understanding the business environment, then moves to developing the brand strategy and architecture, and finally helps identify tactics to deliver the brand. This flow may be a bit more work upfront, but I think it results in a better foundation for success.

The goal of this process is to establish a brand that lives at the intersection of the firm's personality and capabilities, the customers' aspirations and needs, and a defensible competitive position. I also emphasize building and implementing a brand that fosters a long-term loving relationship with the customer base. The market loves fantastic brands and fantastic brands love their customers, potential customers, and non-customers.

Before continuing here are the steps in the process:

1. Business Environmental Assessment
2. SWOT Analysis
3. Target Customer Segment
4. Firm's Personality
5. Big Idea (Courtship)
6. Competitive Differentiation
7. Purpose, Mission, Vision, and Brand Promise
8. Brand Architecture
9. Narratives
10. Brand Personality
11. Positioning Statement
12. Post-Workshop Polishing the Result

It may be surprising that it takes eight steps to get to the brand definition. However, until then the basic information about who the firm is, what it wants to achieve in the world, what it is looking for in a customer, understanding the potential customers' needs, and knowing how it will stand out among other companies isn't known. This information is the basic DNA of the firm. It directly affects the brand definition and later will drive actions.

There will be a tendency to skip steps under the assumption that "we all know this about our firm or offering." However, a good facilitator will question and poke a bit to find out if this is true or bring to light the variety of truths participants are holding. For example, I may ask attendees at the start to take five minutes and write out the purpose of the business. Then I have a few read them aloud to the group. It is always a surprise to the participants when everyone reads something slightly or dramatically different. Don't assume the attendees all have the same perception.

Process Overview:

It begins with a Business Environmental Assessment followed by a SWOT Analysis and then selection of an opportunity. It is beyond the scope of this workbook to inform the reader on how to do an environmental assessment or SWOT analysis, but there are many resources available via the Internet. The worksheets hold a summation of these items.

The next step is to determine the customer type (segment) that will be interested in the selected opportunity and their characteristics, for example, psychosocial, aspirational, emotional, and economic. Then an assessment of the firm's personality identifies where it intersects with the customers' traits. Strong brands intersect in some way with the values, beliefs, or interests of the target market.

If the firm is just starting up, already exists and desires to improve its relevance to the target segment, or needs to revitalize its brand this is the point where the new personality is developed. Also at this point the general description of what the firm can provide that is relevant and meaningful to the customer usually becomes clear. However, the exact specifications for an offering cannot be fully defined yet – that's another workshop. Armed with this information the big idea is created and the company's strategy for competitive differentiation is determined.

Now, it gets more brand-like. From here the company's purpose, vision, mission, and brand promise can be formulated. The brand promise comes from restating the company's purpose or point of differentiation from the point of view of the target customer segment. Developing the Brand Architecture occurs after the brand promise. The promise sits on three to five supporting pillars. These pillars enable the brand promise to become real. Each pillar has an additional eight to ten behaviors and/or operational attributes that support them. The behaviors and attributes are what make the pillars possible. Think of the pillars as strategic and the behaviors and operational attributes as tactics. Take a quick look at sheet 8B.

Once the behaviors and attributes are determined, they each receive a descriptive narrative to illustrate how they come together. The narratives guide the internal development of the brand. This becomes clearer later in the guide - hang in there.

The Positioning Statement comes next. It informs the creation of the value proposition, elevator speech, and the development of key messages. After this the brand's personality is defined. These are the emotional and style elements that support the expression of the brand. These last two exercises are inputs to other workshops. By the way, now it's time for logo and name development.

Remember the example of "fun, hip, and wearing red," from earlier, these items are incorporated into the brand pillars and attributes to help drive the firm's behaviors.

House of Brands or Branded House

The process helps develop a firm's, a product's, or a service's brand; however, first determine if the firm is a "house of brands," or a "branded house." In a house of brands, each offering has its own brand identity and presence in the market. Proctor and Gamble, for example, has thousands of products that each has its own brand identity; they are a house of brands. In a branded house, offerings support the parent company's name and brand. Black and Decker has many products too, but they all carry the parent company name; they are a branded house. There are also companies, like Microsoft, that use a mixture of both.

Note on Brand Revitalization

Before starting a brand revitalization program first solve the business issue that triggered the need; otherwise the outcome will be less than ideal. To put it bluntly, stop the bleeding, find the root cause of the problem, and fix it. The process of fixing the problem concludes with restoring faith in the company and revitalizing the brand.

A Few Notes from the Front Lines

Before I Run a Workshop

Before running a workshop, I sit down with the requesting group's upper management or CEO to find out what the business situation is and what their objectives are. After this I interview key people and/or the management team one-on-one to get a more comprehensive view and a sense of the corporate culture. I will sometimes also interview key accounts or customers to get an outside perspective. I may also do other research to get a deeper sense of how the firm is perceived externally.

Next, I survey the potential participants in the workshop and other key employees to get more information on employee and management perceptions of the firm, the brand, and competitors. What these employees believe influences the market's experience of the brand.

Within the survey are two open-ended questions regarding their perceptions of the present brand. I farm these open-ended questions for their corporate-speak. In the workshop these terms and those like them will become forbidden words. I do this to help participants move towards more active, dynamic, and emotional words – these types of words connect better with the workforce, customers, and the market. The goal is to use powerful words to help support memory and action.

Prior to the workshop, inform all participants not to schedule meetings or calls during the workshop period. Also, tell them they may not use cell phones and computers during sessions. It is best not to surprise people regarding these items on the morning of the workshop.

Two-Days, but…

Ideally, workshops should run for two-days and in some cases three-days, but the ideal is not often available or supported. The workshop duration may be less than two-days, but it means some missing pieces get completed outside of the original workshop. Less than two-days will add more reviews and refinement time to the final report as it goes back around multiple times for input and comments from attendees. Full agreement by everyone on every item rarely happens, at some point a leader has to make a decision or the results just end up weakened to please everyone.

Work in Pairs

Generally, we do our workshops with two facilitators. Team facilitation has proven to be very effective. The lead facilitator is the one who initiates the project. This person has project responsibility and is in charge of customizing and managing the workshop. The second facilitator comes in anytime from the interview stage to just a few days before the session.

The second facilitator assists with the sessions and helps create the post-seminar report. They share the workload during the workshop and while one is facilitating the other is monitoring the participants' engagement level. During breaks or while the small teams are working they refine the workshop as needed. Facilitators should be skilled in team teaching and facilitation, interpersonal communication, rapport building, and knowledgeable of business practices and structures.

If one of the facilitators believes the workshop agenda needs adjusting, for example, due to time or an unexpected surprise, they call an unscheduled break. This gives the facilitators time to discuss, agree, plan, and prepare the materials. If it is a very significant change, they will discuss it with the workshop sponsors and then the attendees; otherwise, they don't mention it.

Significant changes sometimes occur when an issue that can affect the foundation of the business is uncovered. These issues are often not surprises, but have been ignored or denied by the management team. Often these issues are uncovered during the preliminary work. Diplomacy is important in these situations, especially since we generally bring these issues to the surface at the workshop. This process is not about blame, but on learning and moving forward.

Set Up

My preference is to use round tables with only half of the table having chairs and those chairs facing front. If only rectangular tables are available I set them up in a chevron design and slightly offset so everyone can see the front. I put one or two rectangular tables to the back of the room for the leaders to use. Each participant's table has sticky notes, masking tape, pens, and blank paper available as well as a flip chart and easel nearby. I like the flip charts with the sticky upper backs.

A digital projector, screen, and a computer for showing the worksheets and other presentation materials are a necessity. I also, highly recommend using a remote radio frequency or infrared trigger for navigating through the presentation slides. These aren't expensive and provide an added degree of freedom. Try not to use the projector and computer at one of the participant tables; it is less disruptive to the attendees if a separate small table or stand is used.

Early in the workshop the group will be divided into small teams. I don't let people pick their teams, we count off in threes, fours, or fives to create three to five randomly selected teams. Sometimes I will need to balance the teams by individual function even after randomization. I rotate the leadership of the team as much as possible. Don't push people who are indicating they don't want to lead. Be aware that mixing people of different ranks on the same team may not work well in some cultures.

Rules of the Road

After welcoming comments, introductions, and safety information I establish and get agreement on the rules below. Modify these as needed to fit the audience.

- No use of cell phones or computers by attendees during the actual sessions
- Do not schedule meetings during the session times
- Everyone is of equal rank, except the facilitators

he facilitator will not reveal the detail agenda, any exercises, or worksheets before they e needed

- Discussion is encouraged; however the facilitators may stop an exchange and record the item on the "For Future Discussion" list
- Respect each other and treat each other with courtesy
- Each of us is 100% responsible for our actions and reactions
- No one can make you feel or think anything, see rule #6
- Anyone can call a "Time Out," for safety reasons
- Do not make assumptions; ask questions and seek clarity
- If you need something ask; you may get it
- If you are uncomfortable with anything make it known to the facilitators
- All discussions in the workshop stay in the workshop
- Only give feedback when asked. Don't offer feedback unless you first ask if it is wanted. It is okay to say "no" to receiving feedback. The only answer to feedback is "thank you."
- If things get heated or people get triggered it is time for a break
- The facilitators will question and challenge individuals, teams, and the group. It's not personal
- There are no bystanders in the workshop
- We suggest you let go and trust the process.

Where is the Agenda?

I don't show a detailed agenda. In fact, I don't show our materials or detailed agenda to a client ever. It is part of my rules of engagement. There are two reasons for this: 1) the workshop is a discovery process and knowing what is coming constrains creativity, and 2) as was mentioned before, we may change the workshop as needed to adjust for the little surprises that bubble up. If the audience knows our detailed agenda, then we would have to stop, explain ourselves, and sometimes take up valuable time trying to convince people to accept the change.

Everyone Needs a Break

Breaks are about resting and recharging. I like people to have the freedom to get up and leave the room for a short break anytime they need one. However, I inform the attendees not to return and then ask for a recap of what they missed. This is disruptive and slows down the process. They should wait until the next scheduled break to get caught up.

In addition to individual breaks, make sure to take group breaks periodically of no less than fifteen minutes. Lunch breaks should be an hour and are not working sessions. People need time to decompress and rest. Also, be mindful to watch for saturation in the group or a team and if it occurs either change to another activity or call a break - even if not scheduled.

When returning from scheduled breaks, or lunch, take a minute to bring everyone mentally into the room. It can be as simple as everyone taking a deep breath or through a short piece of music. Have paper on a wall where people can write jokes, sayings, or draw graffiti during breaks. The facilitators should refer to one or two from time to time. It can help people vent or express themselves when they don't feel comfortable talking.

Revealing the Statue

"Every block of stone has a statue inside it and it is the task of the sculptor to discover it."
-Michelangelo

Every workshop has the answers in it. Our task as workshop leaders is to help the participants chip away and remove the excess rock to reveal the essence inside. This is not an easy task and it takes time for participants to feel safe so they can open up and contribute within the process and with each other. This is especially important if senior staff is present and in some cultures it may not be possible to mix senior staff with non-managers.

The facilitator's job at the start is to create a "safe container" for the attendees and to provide opportunities for them to gain confidence in moving through this undiscovered country. When they feel safe and confident they can move beyond obvious or easy responses to get to the gold nuggets below. Building a safe container starts with the rules listed earlier and includes:

- Establishing rapport with the group
- Communicating in a non-judgmental or non-punitive way
- Ensuring everyone has an opportunity to be heard
- Supporting an atmosphere of mutual trust and respect
- Helping people feel and experience being empowered

In Workshop 1 – Brand Architecture, my intent is to educate through questioning and discovery, to push beyond the obvious and to arrive at a new more competitive concept that drives the definition of the business and the brand. After the workshop the rough sculpture gets polished before being unveiled to the firm.

At the end of the workshop there is a lot of information to be sifted through and polished. It can take up to eight days to pull all the information together into a draft document. Once the draft is complete, the facilitators meet with a small team from the client to do some additional polishing and then review it with the rest of the attendees and later upper management.

Mix it Up

Don't use just one type of exercise or way to complete the worksheets. Mix it up, use a combination of individual, small team, and whole room activities to get the best result. Provide exercises that let people express themselves using pictures instead of words. Sometimes I have them do a collage or encourage them to draw pictures of the new opportunity, future state, or the brand pillars. However, remember some people will be uncomfortable with drawing so allow them to use words. The bottom line is to vary the activities, be flexible, and help people stay out of guilt or shame if they are having trouble with an activity or way of expressing.

Don't Take the First Answer

Customer segmentation and differentiation in this guide are on one sheet; however, I generally run them as separate one-hour exercises. Other people like them as one sheet. Again, be flexible, if you want to run a section of the worksheet as a separate exercise then try it.

Here is one of the ways I facilitate customer segmentation:

> I will break the group into teams of three to five people and have each team use a flip chart easel and paper to write down how they would segment the market. After 15 minutes, I check in with each group separately to see what they came up with and I ask them to explain the reasons behind the segmentation they created. It is important to keep them focused on being concise.
>
> After hearing how they segmented the market, I remove the flip chart paper and place it to the side, and ask them to start again and try to find a different way to segment the market. I may have them repeat this up to four times. Why repeat the exercise? Because the first two or three are generally obvious, easy, typical, and often the same segments the competitors use. The last one or two attempts often exposes a new paradigm that may yield a more competitive position. Be careful to avoid frustrating and shutting down the participants.

Lastly, I test key areas such as purpose, mission, and differentiation by having them put their competitors' names in front of the statements. If they still read true then I ask them to start again until we find a unique position or strategy or until they decide, what they have is right for them – the Jeff Robinson test.

Riding Off Into the Sunset

Before I close the workshop I review what the group achieved, what the next steps are, who has further actions, and I go over the items on the "For Future Discussion" list (see workshop rules). After answering any questions, I then do a formal closing process that includes restatement of the "discussions in the workshop are confidential" rule and then set the date for the review of the draft final report.

But Wait There's More…

Okay, they have the final report; now what? This is one of the make or break moments, because either they keep the momentum and take the next step or they stop. Therefore, it's important to get commitment before the workshop that the firm will start a planning exercise to map out the next 24 months on the heels of the final report. The planning needs to realistic and factor in what is achievable given the resources and time available.

Focus on developing a balanced plan, where some quick gains can be made while longer term items are underway. Getting change in motion with some quick victories helps build momentum. I suggest focusing during the first phase of implementation on product design, brand marketing, quality, service, and training managers and those that directly touch the customers.

Managers are the most important group in this process; their commitment determines whether the brand will be implemented successfully or not. Management training focuses on how to manage and hire for brand. Why be so aggressive on training managers? Because, management makes the rules, which means they are the priests of the corporate culture.

I highly suggest forming a cross-functional brand team led by Marketing. This team will become the group that will guide the implementation of the brand and provide mentoring to managers and others. Also, while the top-down work is forming, get started on a bottom up effort as well.

The bottom up effort starts after managers are trained. Give them sixty-days to work with their teams to select one item and only one item that they can improve with respect to brand. It must be something that is within their immediate control, can be implemented within six months, and measureable. Recognize and celebrate each completion.

Some teams involved in the "select one item to improve" exercise may find it hard to conceptualize. For these groups it may help if they consider the people that provide them input as vendors and teams they hand-off their output to as customers. The group can then decide on an item based on getting a better input from their vendors or to help their customer (downstream) be more successful. By expressing needs, adaptability, and love upstream and downstream, the internal group can improve the delivery of the external brand.

For All Worksheets

One set of worksheets comes with this guide and the sheets may be ordered as a workbook package for each attendee. The workbook contains all the worksheets, but without the guide content. The pdf and PowerPoint versions of the worksheets are available to all purchasers of the guide at our website. Each sheet is 8.5" x 14" and the block sizes allow for the use of small sticky notes in each block during brainstorming activities. Each download contains two sets of sheets, one with the questions and one without.

The worksheet numbers and block numbers on each sheet make referencing items between sheets easier. In Planning Workshops, we utilize the numbers to create a work breakdown structure for use in developing road maps and project plans. Lastly, the questions in each block are not exhaustive. They are only there to stimulate thinking.

A little note:

Educate the group on asking themselves these two questions during their workday:

 Is what I am about to do going to strengthen or weaken the brand?

 Am I making a conscious choice?

One Last Note Before Jumping In

What we are doing during the first half of this process is actually building up an image or persona of three characters: the firm, the customer, and the competition. Then we take these personas and use them to help define the brand and potentially the offering. Think back to the first page when I mentioned the pictures of the comedian and the singer. Obviously, they have talent – their core competency. Next, they may have decided to strategically focus their talent to meet the needs and style of a specific customer segment. Then they may have created a public persona to fit that market niche – a brand. This is what the worksheets are helping the firm develop.

Worksheet 1 – Business Environment

Business Environment

As stated earlier it is beyond the scope of this workshop to do an Environmental Analysis because of time and resource limitations. This sheet captures the results of an analysis completed earlier for review with the participants.

This worksheet and the SWOT Analysis sheet assess the firm and the environment it lives in. This process culminates with evaluating and selecting an opportunity for the company to pursue in the market. If the selection occurred before the workshop, for example, as part of an earlier strategic planning process, inform the attendees. Avoid the temptation to let them go through opportunity selection to find out if they match the decision already made. It may be very disruptive to the workshop when they find out their choice doesn't count.

Side Trip Back to Houses and Brands

What if the firm operates in a number of different industries or a number of areas within an industry, how does this relate to selecting one opportunity on which to base the brand? This goes back to the earlier question regarding where the company falls on the continuum of "house of brands" to "branded house." In the "house of brands" case, and especially if there is a lot of diversity, each product or service stands alone and can be treated like an individual company with respect to this workshop. In other words, each major offering goes through its own workshop.

A firm that leans heavily towards a "branded house," focuses more on setting its positioning based on the core competencies that all of its products and services share. However, the more diverse the offerings are the more generalized the firm's overall brand may become. If the firm's offerings are linked by similar technologies, styling, or attributes - related diversity, then the brand expression tends to be less generalized. Where on the continuum should a firm be? That's a strategic decision for the company.

Some car manufactures not known for luxury cars have tried to move into the luxury car market. Toyota may have decided that they had a low probability of extending their affordable every person's brand of car into the luxury market, so they created Lexus – house of brands. KIA is taking a different approach. They are going to try to expand into the luxury car market under their current name and brand – branded house. It remains to be seen if the upscale consumer market will support Kia's choice.

Brand is a Business Strategy

The thesis "Brands are behaved," may need a little more clarification. The brand is an expression of a business strategy or market position that supports a business objective. Achieving the brand strategy occurs through organizational structures and a set of operational, design, pricing, marketing, communications, and other activities. This worksheet and the one addressing SWOT helps set the foundation for creating the brand strategy.

Question Their Conclusions

As a facilitator of the workshop it is important to gently question the participants on the potential accuracy of the information contained on this and the next worksheets. Get a feel for what is an assumption or pure speculation verses a conclusion based on some real data and analysis.

It may be helpful to ask questions like:

> How do you know that's true?
>
> What would it mean if the opposite was true?
>
> How would a competitor respond to that?
>
> What indicates the gap in the market actually exists?
>
> Is there a time limit to get to market and what happens if the deadline is missed?
>
> Does the customer have any latent or unarticulated needs not being met?
>
> Has something happened in the environment to cause the nature of the firm to change?

Of course it is the nature of business to operate with an incomplete or less than perfect set of data, and although I encourage good solid research and analysis each company decides for itself how much it needs. Some will operate on gut feel and others will want to get blood tests and finger prints from everyone. Try to find a compromise between the wild pioneer and the one paralyzed by analysis.

During the workshop it's not unusual to uncover significant business issues. Some groups may be in full denial of any business problems or blind and deaf to things that challenge their reality. Others may be suffering from an inferiority complex or functioning out of fear. Gentle guiding questions and hypothetical situations are often the best way to expand their view. Of course, sometimes direct assertive statements may be required to shake the group up enough to address the issue. When being direct remember people occasionally follow Newton's third law, "For every reaction there is an equal and opposite reaction."

Worksheet 1 - Business Environment

1. Core Competency

What is/are the firm's core competency or competencies? Are any of the competencies unique in the market? Are these competencies relevant today and to what group? How difficult would it be for another firm to duplicate these competencies or render them obsolete?

2. Underserved Segment

Is there an underserved customer segment in the market? Are there any unarticulated or articulated customer needs not being met? Is a major competitor not responding to customer's complaints or desires? Are customers expressing a frustration with the status quo? How big is this underserved market? Are there any companies attempting to address this market?

3. Market Gap

Is there a gap in technology, process, or practice in the market that would provide a viable opportunity? What would the firm or offering need to do to fill this gap? Would this filler be easy to duplicate? Is there something from another industry that could fill this gap?

4. Relevant Economic Conditions

What are the regional, national, or international conditions that either contribute or inhibit the growth of the market? How will the firm take advantage or mitigate these conditions? Over the next five-years is there a possible economic or trade condition that could help or threaten the firm? What would the early indicators be and what would the firm's potential response be?

5. Emerging Trends, Regulations, Issues, or Threats to Market or Industry

Over the next 5 years are there any emerging trends, regulations, opportunities, issues, or threats to the market and/or the customer base. For example, government regulations to install new technologies or creation of new restrictions, new taxes, entry of disruptive technologies, or environmental conditions. Does a potential opportunity or threat exists for only a finite period of time?

Worksheet 2 – SWOT Analysis

It's a Four Dimensional Assessment

The SWOT Analysis is the business school go to when working on business strategy; however, it is beyond this guide to instruct on how to do a SWOT Analysis. There are a lot of references available via the Internet.

The sheet has two major parts. Part one is an assessment on the four SWOT dimensions – two externally and two internally focused. The second is analysis, which ends in selecting an opportunity that will increase the long-term health and viability of the business. This sheet is primarily about sharing, it assumes the analysis has been done prior to the workshop. However, completing the SWOT during the workshop does occur from time-to-time.

Recently, I altered the SWOT structure for workshops at large companies by adding a few extra bits. Under Strength, Weakness and Threats I have the group look both internally and externally. This can help reveal some additional information. For example, sometimes departments within the firm may be as threatening (uncooperative) as outside forces or resistant to change.

The greatest amount of analysis activity centers on evaluating the list of opportunities to determine the one to pursue. After selecting the opportunity the firm needs to re-examine the other dimensions to ascertain what may need to be strengthened, eliminated, improved, or added to in order to best support the chosen opportunity.

Questions to think about:

- What behaviors will support the selected opportunity?
- If the firm has a brand, what does the Brand SWOT look like?
- What will make the chosen opportunity highly relevant and meaningful to customers?
- Does the selected opportunity enable the firm to establish a mid- to long-term competitive barrier?

Business Objectives and Strategies

Although these worksheets center on brand they can also help build the firm's operational business objectives. Objectives are outcomes based on time bound measureable goals (search the Internet for information on SMART Goals). For example, "The business will increase earnings by 10% within three years." A goal does not state how it is achieved. If you find an objective contains words like and, by or through it indicates a strategy is included in the objective.

A strategy is a broad statement that states how the firm will achieve its goal. Each objective may have one to five major strategies. Typically each department will have goals and strategies that support the overall business strategies. Each strategy will generally have two to five major tactics associate with it. As stated earlier, brand or positioning is a business strategy.

One group's business strategy may be another group's objectives. Considering the top-down structure of a business and its various departments, often the strategy of the group the team reports to can be re-phrased into a team's objective. The team's objective then drives the creation of their strategies and tactics. This cascading process of one person's strategy becoming another's objective helps vertically integrate the organization.

During the planning workshop this cascade is built up in a stepwise fashion. Use a coding method to identify what strategies, tactics, and objectives are associated. For example:

Objective 1
    Strategy A
        Tactic 1
        Tactic 2
        Tactic 3
    Strategy B
        Tactic 1
        Tactic 2
        Tactic 3

Objective 2
    Strategy A
        Tactic 1
        Tactic 2
        Tactic 3
    Strategy B
        Tactic 1
        Tactic 2
        Tactic 3

Objective 2
    Strategy A
        Tactic 1
        Tactic 2
        Tactic 3
    Strategy B
        Tactic 1
        Tactic 2
        Tactic 3

Objective 3
    Strategy A
        Tactic 1
        Tactic 2
        Tactic 3
    Strategy B
        Tactic 1
        Tactic 2
        Tactic 3

In this example tactic 2 for strategy B under objective 3 would be referred to as 3.B.2. This coding is helpful when doing road mapping and eventually when building a Work Breakdown Structure. It is possible for a tactic to be applicable to more than one strategy.

Worksheet 2 – SWOT Analysis

1. Strengths	2. Weaknesses
List the items that the firm does well internally, that is, what customers can't see, and list what the company does well that customers can see. Of the items listed identify which of these creates a competitive advantage for the firm? Rank these in order of importance to the firm's success.	List the items within the firm that are weak or result in less than optimum operation? List the items customers and the market would perceived as the firm's weaknesses? Rank these in order of impact to the success of the firm?

3. Opportunities	4. Threats
What opportunities exist in the near-, mid-, and long-term that could provide value to the firm? Do one or more of these opportunities exist where there are no competitors? Could the firm open up a new product or service category? Is their a window of opportunity, if yes, how long will it be open? Rank these opportunities in order of potential return or advantage to the firm.	What does or will threaten the firm from the outside (competitor, supplier, or government actions)? What threats exist from within the company? Which ones have or will have, significant impact on the firm's chance of being successful.

5. Strengths	What items should be left at their current level of strength and which ones should be made even stronger? How do you determine which is which?
6. Weaknesses	What items should be strengthened and which ones should be eliminated? How do you determine which is which?
7. Opportunities	What opportunity should be pursued and why? This will be the reference point for the rest of the worksheets.
8. Threats	What should be done to reduce the risk to the firm or its offerings by these threats?

There is some redundancy in questions and blocks when the entire set of sheets is examined. The redundancy is to compensate for workshops that use a shortened process and it also provides opportunities to step back and refine previous answers based on new information developed through the process.

Worksheet 3 – Target Customer Segment

"All you need is love…"

What would it be like if the business-customer relationship was built on a healthy loving foundation? No co-dependency, exploitation, or abuse; only a true heart-to-heart connection. The exchange of goods for money (exchange of rings) being a symbol of a mutual commitment to love. How would that feel? What would the firm be like if it was built on this basis?

It does sound weird, but does it ring true on some level? What would the customer retention rates be if the customer and the firm were in this type of relationship? It may appear on the surface that the customer only wants the physical thing – candy and flowers, but what they really want is connection and support in continuing to grow? Because business is always between people it doesn't matter if it's B2C or B2B "love is all we need." Don't be afraid to show unconditional love within the firm and with customers. Unconditional love does not mean lack of healthy boundaries. One does not have to give away the store just because you love a customer.

This and the next couple of worksheets are like a survey for a dating service. The results help define what the firm wants in a perspective customer and what a potential customer wants from the firm. The understanding of each other's needs forms the basis of the business love bond. All this information feeds the eventual design of the brand architecture.

Questions to consider:

- What elements should the brand have that would bring the firm and customer closer together?
- What items or things would irritate or drive a wedge between the firm and the customer?
- What effect should or shouldn't the customer's personality have on the firm's brand?

I am the Same – I am Unique

People like to form community. It is part of our hardwiring. Whether it is sports, scrapbooking, comic books, wearing a reptile on a polo shirt, or being a Linux programmer we all want to affiliate with something, especially a winning team or successful brand.

We love to show our colors –our affiliation, to signal to others like us that we belong to the same group and to show those that aren't like us that they don't belong. Luxury brands are great examples of this. Motorcycle owners too; they wave to each other but not to moped riders. When developing the brand consider how the firm will support the formation of a healthy community. Consider the difference between a healthy and unhealthy community from the view of someone inside and outside the group.

Equally as strong as the need for being part of a community or group is the desire to be recognized as unique and special. When a firm creates its brand, it needs to understand how it will support these two drives: individuality verses group identity and customization verses commonality. How will the brand make the customer feel special and recognize them as being part of a select group?

Experience at Achievement

Block 3A.4 is often hard for some people to answer. The focus is not on the item but on what the item lets the customer experience and feel. The answers should be focused on the emotional experienced or the state of being achieved. In other words, "I experience being rich," is okay, but expressing what "being rich" feels like generates more insight. For example, it may be an experience of feeling safe and secure.

Don't push people to hard on this one, they may feel uncomfortable expressing in this way with the group. Even though they are speaking for a customer, in reality, they are subconsciously speaking about themselves. For that reason, if possible, it is best to interview selected customers about this item too.

Got Linked?

A brand symbolizes what the firm can do to relieve a customer's tension, conflict, barrier, or to help them achieve an aspiration. Worksheet 3A explores the customers' needs and attempts to determine their source. Knowing the source enables the firm to position the brand as the solution or vehicle to relieve tension or help attain an aspiration.

Ideally, successful linkage between brand, problem, and solution means that when the potential customer experiences a need the firm's name pops into their heads as the only answer, or at least as one of the top three companies to contact. This is called being "top of mind." Firms that are not "top of mind," will find it difficult to compete against those that are in the list. Creating linkage is one of the major functions of the brand's promotional campaign.

Words that Sing

Worksheet 3B is about identifying the language of the customer segment relative to the opportunity. This excludes jargon and abbreviation; neither of which creates much cerebral intensity. Cerebral intensity makes marketing and sales messages sing. It helps the potential customer attach emotion and sensation to the firm's brand.

To attain cerebral intensity, use words that create emotions, sounds, feelings, and images in the mind of the listener. For example, observe the difference between "proven" and "combat-ready." Which creates more imagery, sounds, and feelings in the brain? The right words help build rapport, communicate the brand effectively, propel getting to "top of mind," and help speed up the sales process. Note: Combat-ready works here only if it's what the customer is seeking to attain.

Worksheet 3A – Target Customer Segment

1. Firm's Dating Preference

What type of customer is the best match for the firm? Describe in terms like economic, social, psychological, and motivational traits or attributes for a typical customer. In other words, describe the firm's dream date or mate? Why are these characteristics important to the company?

2. Customer Desires & Worries

What does the customer desire to achieve or have relief from? What keeps them up at night that they can see. What would keep them up at night that they don't see? What do they want to achieve with respect to the selected opportunity? What do these customers value and believe?

3. Customers' Dating Preferences

What does the average customer in this segment desire of their match - vendor? What is important to them in a relationship? What attributes do they seek in a mate and what characteristics do they avoid? What will they experience if the firm is their ideal mate?

4. Experience at Achievement

What will the customer experience if they achieved their goal or get relief from a situation? Describe this as an outcome based on utility and in emotional, social, and aspirational terms. Can the market be divided into two or three distinct customer types, that is, segments?

5. Motivators

What motivates the customer to start dating (investigating) and eventually marrying (purchasing from) the firm? Do any of these point to items that the firm needs to created or strengthen?

6. Barriers

What prevents or inhibits the customer from dating and/or marrying the firm? How will the firm over come this resistance; other than bringing candy and flowers to the date (changing the price)?

Worksheet 3B – Target Customer Segment

What active, dynamic, illustrative, and/or emotional language best describes the average customer in the segment?

1. Active	2. Dynamic	3. Illustrative	4. Emotional

5. Describe the customer's (customer is an individual or a firm) personality using psychosocial attributes?
   It may be helpful to answer these "What" questions and then explore how the answers can help describe the average customer's personality.

   What celebrity would the customer be?   What foods would they eat?
   What sports would he/she watch?   What type of movies would they enjoy?
   What car would they drive?   What would they like to do in their free time?
   What animal would she/he be?   What do they aspire to?

Worksheet 4A – Firm's Personality Defined

Overview

"Do not determine their virtue from their manifesto; watch and listen to gain a true assessment,"
- Yitzhock ben Yoel.

Virtue is the set of behaviors that demonstrate one is living to a high standard of moral, ethical, and social conduct. It's generally something we respect in others and aspire to maintain in ourselves. We trust people who act with integrity and virtue and we like doing business with them too.

It takes years to built trust and integrity in the market and it can take seconds to tear it down. To put it differently, it takes years to build a solid brand and seconds to lose its market value if it stops acting with virtue. How a firm behaves when things go bad speaks volumes about its collective character and integrity. Consider how BP first handled the oil spill in the Gulf of Mexico in April 2010 and consider what impact this had on their brand worldwide.

Strong brands, good brands, and great brands consistently exhibit integrity and virtue. These companies go beyond writing corporate manifestos about honesty, integrity, quality, ethics, people first, customer-driven, etc. to teaching and living these attributes every day and in every action. Acting in conflict to its manifesto increases the likelihood the firm will fall short of reaching its maximum potential. Do customers prefer a low price from a company that lies and cheats or would they pay a higher price to work with people they trust?

There are a series of blocks on the worksheet that help assess what the firm believes and values and whether it holds true to these in their day-to-day operations. This is not about looking to blame or to judge, but to bring awareness of any disconnects between what is desired and what is practiced. Correcting disconnects strengthens the brand.

It is also about finding out how the firm consciously or unconsciously prioritizes their values. For example, is shipping on time more important than quality? Does always showing a positive spin to the world overshadow truth and transparency? Getting this order of precedence clear supports the creation and maintenance of the brand. It is part of conscious decision-making and good management.

Values and Disconnects

In the section on values, the focus is on determining the firm's principles or standards of behavior with regard to what is important in life within and surrounding the company. The questions about ranking and rating help illuminate any possible disconnects in the firm. Disconnects can become festering wounds within a corporate culture and brand.

Disconnects occur when the firm repeatedly violates its beliefs or values and/or causes employees to choose to be in conflict with their personal integrity. People will generally try to relieve this conflict, or stress by quitting, causing disruption, reducing productivity, wrecking the customer experience, disassociating from themselves at work, or potentially doing physical damage to the company. Thus disconnects create ripples of instability in the firm and a loss of respect in management. If these go on long enough they may become embedded in the firm's processes and culture either formally or informally.

It's the job of management to correct these disconnects, that is, to "fix the brand." Management creates and owns the corporate culture, not the employees. In other words, those that set the rules establish the culture. I suggest first having management apologize for the creating the situation and then go after correcting the situation as firmly, fairly, and timely as possible in order to start rebuilding brand equity.

We use rankings and ratings to help identify potential weak areas and to stimulate future discussion and change. Facilitators need to work gently and constructively during and after the workshop to help management fix disconnects. It can take weeks to a few years to overcome a firmly embedded integrity issue.

In the compromise block we begin exploring the operational and behavioral limits of the firm with respect to its day-to-day activities. How do the answers in this block impact the selected opportunity and the target customer segment? A similar exercise is run for items that are sacred to the firm.

What we hold sacred is truly one of the defining items of the brand. If the firm holds concepts like contemporary design, environmental responsibility, or affordable living as sacred this will become the touchstone that guides the viewpoint and choices of the company. Sacred items are part of the brand architecture and generally show up as one or more pillars.

Why is there all this stuff on values, compromising, etc.? Simply it is a way to shine a mirror on the firm and give it a chance to become more aware of itself and see where it can improve so they can be a better match for the customers.

Heroes and Allies

We use the heroes block to begin assessing the character traits of the firm, and later with other inputs, to help inform the choice of sensory elements for expressing the brand. How do these traits align with the target customer segment?

Allies are those non-customers that believe in the firm; provide aid, and who the firm has a relationship with and obligation to support. They can also help multiple the effects of the firm's promotional efforts by echoing the company's messages.

Worksheet 4A – Firm's Personality

The primary purpose of these blocks relates to the creation or repair of the firm's culture. Culture is a major factor in band delivery. These blocks can help in constructing the firm's heroes journey.

1. Values

What are the firm's values - principles or standards of behavior? What value, or values, would the firm choose to go out of business over then violate? Rank the values in order of importance to the firm and indicate if these values are consistently demonstrated. How does the ranking impact the firm's success? How will managers and employees learn about and demonstrate these values?

2. Compromises

What items would the firm never compromise on? What items would the firm compromise on that customer would see? What items would the firm compromise on that customers would never see? How do these answers relate to 4A.1? Think of it this way, back in the kitchen, where customer can't see, a piece of fried fish falls to the floor. Is it okay to put it back in the fryer and then serve it?

3. Sacred

What does the firm hold as sacred? Consider this from many different angles, for example: human resources, design, sourcing, company culture, aesthetics, quality, or beliefs. Rank these from most sacred to least sacred. How do these items impact success? How are these items incorporated in the firm's culture and processes? Think about what Apple or BMW may hold sacred and how it helps them.

4. Heroes

Whether real, fictional, or mythological who are the firm's heroes? What are the positive and negative traits of these characters? Why are these characters important to the firm? What role do they play? Are there conflicts between characters? How does the firm emulate their behaviors? Are these the heroes the firm wants to be like? If not, who are the characters and what are their traits?

5. Allies

Who or what are the firm's allies? This could be a person, company, agency, or key item that helps the firm be successful? What makes them allies? How does the firm support them and/or show gratitude? How do they support the firm? What does the firm have in common with them? Why do they want to join the firm on its quest to change the world?

6. The Firm's Offer to the World

How does the firm benefit mankind, the world, a region, or a locale? Other than to make money, why is the firm in business? How does the firm improve the human condition? What would future historians say about the firm and how it impacted the world?

Worksheet 4B – Firm's Personality Described

Words to Lose and Words to Use

"Hundreds of butterflies flitted in and out of sight like short-lived punctuation marks in a stream of consciousness without beginning or end."   - Haruki Murakami.

Business Version: "I saw a lot of butterflies today. "

Language impacts us in many overt and subtle ways. It can expand our thinking or contract it like a punctured balloon. Sometimes it can empower and rally to action; other times it can arrive tired, worn out, or stillborn. It can sound like the harmony of an orchestra or a staccato of a politician's measured and stilted words. It can be full of jargon or light, lyrical and full of life. Words matter and the most memorable phrases are ones that touch us on many different levels: visual, auditory, emotional, physical, spiritual, etc.

During my workshops I introduce people to the simple three-brain model; reptilian, limbic, and cognitive parts of the brain. This is a bit overly simplistic, but it does the job. The reptilian brain, the oldest, is focused on survival: eating, breathing, reproduction, etc. When politicians and some non-profits put out messages that are heavy on the next threat to survival or the family they are appealing to this part of the brain. If the reptilian is activated successfully it will over-ride the limbic and cognitive processes. This is why a logical rebuttal to messaging on "threats to children" rarely work.

The limbic system is focused on our emotions and our unconscious beliefs and drivers. This is the part of the brain where most decisions are made. The take away here is simple; decisions are almost never made by the cognitive parts of the brain. The cognitive areas are great with facts and data and do well to help justify a decision, but generally, this section isn't making the decision. In fact, the cognitive brain will do its best to create a story to put all the pieces (external stimuli and internal processing) together in a way that will appear to make sense, even if in reality it doesn't.

What this means is we use emotional words to carry our messages while also appealing to the potential customer's basic motivations or drivers. Then we provide facts and data to help their cognitive brain support closing the deal. We let illustrative language and story carry our messaging into their long-term memory. However, there must be a truth in this to work; otherwise, you will leave the person with a bitter after-taste that may reduce brand strength. Recall the discussion of virtue earlier.

We are not excluding images or video at all. But everything starts with the words. Many people get worried that we are saying that every message or brochure needs to be a novel. This isn't the case; we are looking for an economy of powerful words, analogies, and metaphors as well as imagery and sound. Our goal is tight motivational and memorable communication.

Forbidden Words

Prior to workshop we do a survey of the participants and others to gather some of their perceptions. Within this survey are one or two open-ended questions about the firm and its brand. These answers are farmed for their recurring words, corporate speak, jargon, clichés, and over used terms. These terms go on a large chart titled "Forbidden Words," or words-to-lose. These are banned during the workshop. Typically, these are words and phrases like world-class, efficiency, shareholder value, premium, leverage, and performance. When the words go up on the board, some people may get a bit uncomfortable. This is normal. They are initially confused because they don't know how to talk about the firm or its offerings without these words.

Forbidden words are the ones that don't light up the brain very well. They speak only to the cognitive part of the brain, offering little to the limbic and reptilian; therefore, they yield little cerebral intensity. It is like eating food without any taste, smell, or texture.

This worksheet is about finding the words to use. Words that can breath, move and motivate people to connect with, and support, the firm. An exercise I sometimes use has the participants draw a picture of the firm's future successful state. No words are allowed on the image. They then explain their picture within a small team. Next they write as many one to two word phrases as they can in three minutes to describe the outcome or feelings symbolized by the image.

Lastly they compare lists with the others and create a master list of the twelve most active, dynamic, Illustrative, and emotional words. All the teams report out and place their lists on the wall or board. These are the words to use; the ones that will help bring the brand to life.

Complete the worksheet as a group activity with people calling out words or try the exercise described above.

Simple Enough a Ten-Year Old will Understand

The last part of the worksheet asks the participants to write a description of the firm's personality such that a ten-year old would understand it. This helps drive out the jargon and corporate speak and yields a creative, tighter, and more powerful paragraph. Corporate speak is just silly cognitive crap, I mean jargon.

One More Disconnect

During interviews conducted before the workshop we asked interviewees to define their key or strategic words or terms. This is especially important when the department head or C-suite is interviewed. We will then ask the managers who report to these leaders to define some of the strategic words or terms their boss uses. This can be very revealing.

The definitions are then compared to determine if there are any "strategic vocabulary disconnects." Strategic vocabularies are terms used to communicate the direction and actions of the firm, for example, when a leader says, "We are going to increase our rate of *innovation*." Often there's an assumption that everyone has the same definition for terms like "innovation." What if the people, who are charged with making the firm more innovative, don't have the same definition as the leader? Not having the same meaning to key terms can lead to misunderstanding, frustration, tension, and failure without any awareness by the parties as to why things didn't work. This is how a vocabulary disconnect causes damage.

What is the cure? We ask leaders to define these key terms over and over again for a period of time when launching a new initiative. This covers all channels, for example, speeches, print and electronic materials. We encourage their direct reports to follow the same pattern too. This includes communicating with customers as well. Clarity can help create powerful outcomes.

During the workshop it is a good practice to ask people to define key or strategic terms as they come up. Therefore at the start of the workshop explain about vocabulary disconnects so participants know why they are going to be periodically quizzed about their terms.

Worksheet 4B – Firm's Personality

What active, dynamic, illustrative, and/or emotional language best describes the average customer in the segment?

1. Active	2. Dynamic	3. Illustrative	4. Emotional

5. Using as many of the words above, write a paragraph that describes the firm to a ten-year old.

Worksheet 5 – Courtship

A Little More Love...

> "Win customers for life. Delight the customer. The customer is first. Make the customer feel special. It starts with the customer and ends with the customer. We pride ourselves on having great customer relationships."

All of these taglines are common in B2B and B2C enterprises, yet they don't truly touch on the essence of what is underneath. Perhaps as business people we are afraid to use the right term – it can be scary to use the L-word, "Love."

A number of firms say, "We love our customers," but for some companies the sentence is missing an unspoken insidious addition; "*...as long as they are purchasing from us.*" This is conditional love. If they stop buying we don't love them anymore. The firm may even feel angry, rejected, abandoned, inadequate, and/or fearful. The phrase "it's not personal; it's business," is a fallacy, everything is personal; companies are made of people. Take some time to research co-dependent relationships before doing a workshop and be open to seeing how it gets played out in the firm.

What would it be like if the sentence, "We love our customers," is changed to, "We are in love with our customers?" This turn of phrase is to denote an unconditional love that seeks connection whether a transaction occurs or not. It is also an understanding that by expressing love in all dealings, even when a purchase doesn't occur, the goodwill and positive energy projected by the "love-firm," may set up a better future state with the individual and/or those they influence. What goes around comes around often is true. Minimally it just makes the world a happier place.

Unconditional love does not mean subsuming the needs and feelings of the firm to the customer or vice versa. It requires loving the person as they are; their essence, as an equal. It includes supporting each other in growing and prospering in healthy ways. Sometimes it's loving their essence even when their ways and yours don't align enough to have any type of relationship.

Like all relationships a business can't truly practice unconditional love unless it first has unconditional love for itself. Can a firm express love for its customers if it doesn't express love within its four walls? Our advice is to model inside the company the behaviors customers should experience at the front of the store.

This is one of the contexts to keep in mind as the workshop continues – inside behaviors drive the outside expression of the brand. This helps create a business people want to connect with and help build.

Some items to consider when later formulating the firm's brand behaviors, or culture:

- Engage fully with each other - be 100% focus
- Practice open and honest communication from a place of love and empathy

- Speak one's truth from a place of personal responsibility and integrity
- Listen to understand, in contrast to listening to formulate a reply
- Realize that everyone is doing the best they can at every given moment, and when they know more and/or are more aware they will do better.
- Hold each other and the customers 100% responsible for their own actions, feelings, and reactions.
- Expresses one's concerns, hurts, and boundaries in a healthy way and support others doing the same
- Embrace differences; it opens the mind and is good for business
- Foster trust – forgive freely
- Never compromise the individual's or the firm's integrity
- Contribute to building mutually supporting relationships
- Break off relationships that aren't healthy
- Be free to be who you are
- Cultivate patience, understanding, and flexibility in dealings.
- Build community
- Love for the joy of loving – no strings, no expectations, no guilt or shame, and no conditions

Intersection and Commonality

This section is a further exploration of what was started on earlier sheets. We tend to form relationship easier with those whose beliefs, personality, values, desires, etc intersect with our own. We may also bond over a common experience or interest; however some bonds carry a potential negative shadow. For example, a bond formed over a trauma or dependency. Avoid creating dependent customers; they eventually revolt.

Just for Them – A Special Gift

When the firm intersects and understands its target customers then it can deliver them a gift that is deeply meaningful and memorable. The gifts are the firm's offerings. Great brands design offerings that meet the customers' articulated and some of their key unarticulated (latent) needs. Delivering on unarticulated needs can generate fantastic customer loyalty and differentiation.

Suitors

This section begins the discussion that will lead to identifying the sustainable competitive differentiator. It may be worthwhile to consider Porter's Forces here as well. The objective is to think about the elements of the brand that could render the competitor invisible to a loyal customer.

Worksheet 5 – Courtship

1. Intersection & Commonality

What do the firm and the customer segment have in common; personality, values, beliefs, desires, aspirations, needs, etc that will form a basis for a long-term relationship?

2. Just for Them

If a typical customer could specify an offering that would meet all of their stated and unstated needs with respect to the selected opportunity, what would this offering be like? Describe this starting from first use through last? What would the customer say is their ideal company with respect to the selected opportunity. Focus on the key concepts and not on all the details. Will meeting these customer needs violated the beliefs, values, or goals of the company

3. Suitors

How are you going to ward off other suitors for your customers' affection and business? What barriers can you erect to block competitors? What allies can you call for help? How will you be able to tell if a suitor has come calling on your customer?

4. Show the Love

How is the firm going to demonstrate their love and caring for the customers? Consider this from the moment the customer makes contact, through purchase, use, and the retirement of the product or service. Don't list all the details, focus on the specific definitive items or actions. What will make this relationship meaningful to both parties? How will the firm and the customer support each other in their learning, growth and success? How will the relationship evolve over time? What are the key brand moments, the proof points that are meaningful events or items in the relationship.

Worksheet 6 – Differentiation

Where are we?

By this time it is easy to start getting a bit lost and confused. SWOTs, dating, and love, how is this all going to come together? Trust me, I'm a marketer, it will coalesce into a coherent whole. Let's take stock:

1. The business environment is understood
2. The major items the firm needs to strengthen, eliminate, and keep have been identified
3. Thought has been given to how to mitigate or prepare for threats and risks
4. An opportunity has been selected
5. The market or target customer segment that aligns with the opportunity has been determined
6. An assessment has been made of the target market based on their beliefs, needs, desires, etc.
7. The firm's personality and beliefs haves been determined and tested to see if they intersect with those of the customer
8. A start has been made on the offering for the opportunity
9. The differentiation strategy is starting to become visible
10. The brand positioning and key messaging are starting to germinate

There has been a lot of activity in a relatively short time. The foundation is starting to look pretty solid. Now it is time to start framing the building, and getting the walls and roof up. The next step is to complete the differentiation strategy.

Differentiation Aids Survival

Darwin brought back many specimens from his trips and the ones from the Galapagos were the most famous. Many years after the trip experts re-examined a number of his Galapagos bird specimens and determined that many that look different actually were from the same family of finch. Over eons, groups of finches physically adapted to different food sources.

Nature, the great free market, used natural selection to shape each group of finches to best fit their food source, or niche. This shaping or differentiation enabled the finches to minimize potential conflict between groups and others. Businesses are the same; they attempt to minimize competition for customers by differentiating from their competitors. In addition, differentiation is not static, it needs to evolve in response to changes in the customer segment as well as to adapt to pressure from competitors (predators).

Unlike finches, business can decide to strike a balance between specialization by form, fit, and function and flexibility and adaptability. This balance helps prevent waking up to find the customer base gone. It is best to move in sync with the food source. Also, switching to another type of food is better than staying with dwindling supplies. This is not in conflict with loving a customer; it ensures there will always be a customer to love. We can still love are ex-customers as we begin to develop relationships with a new segment. We have an unlimited capacity to love.

Differentiation Effects Margin

Differentiation can come in a number of forms; for example, price, features or functions, outcome, or values and beliefs. Competing on price generally means the firm's and its competitor's offerings are viewed by the market as essentially the same. When this occurs one firm will decide to differentiate by being the lowest priced. This also means having the lowest margins. Differentiating with additional features, functions, or lower risk (a type of feature) in contrast to the competitor's offering supports a higher price relative to price positioning. As a general category, toothpaste is a good example of differentiation by feature. Toothpastes all have the same basic function and the only thing that competitors can differ on are things like taste, texture, whitening, paste color, and packaging. Of course, some brands of toothpaste compete on lowest price.

The next up on the value verses differentiation ladder is outcome. For example, a luxury brand is built and positioned to support a market segment that wants to indicate to themselves and others that they have reached a level of success or exclusivity that few can match. The more a product supports this idea over its competition the higher the price and margin it can command.

The highest value generated by differentiation is by attaching to something of deep meaning (based in values and beliefs) to the customer segment. Owning the product is a symbol of what they hold dear or believe. For example, an environmentalist who buys an electric car or someone committed to only buying from stores that support fair trade and organic foods. This commands the highest level of loyalty with the customer and the best margins relative to a competitor not positioning in this way.

Between two firm's competing on the deep meaning strategy, the one that attaches more strongly to the customers' belief or adds an additional significant differentiator through outcome or feature will generally received the higher market share. This goes for those competing on outcome, they can add feature or price differentiation too.

The best differentiators are those that create a significant barrier to entry, that is, some element that is difficult to duplicate by competitors and other potential predators. The brand identity helps potential customers recall the firm's sustainable competitive difference and how it relates to the customer's need or desire (remember linkage).

Know the Competitors

"Our Fly Smart philosophy is about investing only on those points of differentiation that pay for themselves, that earn a revenue premium commensurate with what it costs us to provide..."
- Gerard Arpey, CEO American Airlines 2004-2011

"You need to understand the market, know how you can differentiate yourself in it, and grasp the price and the functional differentiation competitive points that are going to allow you to be disruptive." - Audrey MacLean, Entrepreneur

It is important to understand how the competitors are differentiating themselves and, if possible, why they selected this strategy in order to minimize conflict in the market. Some companies differentiate by filling customers unarticulated needs, another may take advantage of a new technology, and still others may use customer service or lower prices to carve out their space.

Within a product category, such as cars or lawnmowers, a firm may try to find a feature, function, emotion, or idea that is important to a customer that isn't being differentiate on by other competitors. When such an attribute is found the firm may decide to "own the attribute," that is, to become synonymous with the item. For example, Volvo has established itself over decades of consistent behavior, investment, and promotion as the car that means safety; it owns "top of mind" in his category. It would be very hard for another car company to dislodge Volvo from this position.

From the two quotes above you can see two distinctly different philosophies on differentiation. The quote from Gerard Arpey shows that American Airlines wants to differentiate only on items that generate revenue. If it doesn't bring in more money above their base offering then it isn't worth doing. The common language would be, "The feature must buy its way on the product," or in this case the airplane. Causing a step change or disruption in the market is not their objective.

In contrast, Audrey MacLean would add a feature, function, or benefit to cause a disruption, that is, to alter the way the consumer purchases and/or uses or interacts with the product. This is an attempt to "change the game." If successful, it can render competitors obsolete or a shadow of their former selves. Disruption is a strategy centered on out flanking, surprising and crushing, in contrast to grazing together in the same pasture and eating slightly different plants.

When Apple saw the answer to the mp3 music player market was vertical integration, combining the player and the store to buy the songs individually or as an album, they disrupted both the existing player market and the music industry. This affected Real-Networks, Sony, Rio, and others – it change the customers' purchasing behavior.

A firm's differentiation strategy can be found in such places as their press releases, advertising, packaging, executive statements or interviews, R&D spending allocations, merger activity, annual reports, and new product announcements. It also helps to talk to customers and find out what products they buy and why. This is one area that can't be kept secret. One or more participants of the workshop should be tasked with gathering some of this research prior to the workshop.

The Firm's Differentiation Strategy

There isn't much more to say about differentiation that hasn't already been said in this guide; however, three items need to be emphasized. First, don't accept the team's first couple of answers on differentiation. Acknowledge them and their work, discuss the items briefly, and then have the teams try again; perhaps two or three times. The last one may reveal a hidden gem or two of significant value. Second, once the strategy is determined then test it by reading it with the name of each major competitor. If it sounds true then start again, unless the team wants to compete on the same item. Lastly, check if it is a sustainable competitive advantage. Is it easily copied or difficult to overcome or out flank?

Future History

Future histories are fun, time consuming, and insightful. The future history is a device for establishing a description of the firm's future success state. We typically select a date twenty years in the future and tell attendees that all obstacles were overcame. It seems two decades is enough for most people to accept the premise.

Generally, this activity is done as a separate worksheet, but for this guide we combined it with the differentiation strategy materials. It can also be moved to after the Purpose worksheet. However, I like it here because it can reveal the purpose, mission, and vision as a natural by-product.

I tell attendees to write Future Histories of about three to six paragraphs and then to share them with their team. Next, the team writes a "best of" that they will share with the room. Before the team sharing I may hand out a tip sheet to help them create their history. The tip sheet will ask them to touch on the customers' view, competitors' impact, suppliers, etc., to help round out the picture. Some people may be uncomfortable with writing, that's okay, let them draw a picture. The creation of the "to-be" condition is one of the first steps in doing road mapping, or long-term planning.

Worksheet 6 – Differentiation

1. Competitors' Differentiation

Who are the top competitors and what are they doing to differentiate themselves? What are the key benefits of their offerings and what type of customers are they trying to attract? What issues, desires, needs, etc. have the top competitors associated with their brand? What emotions do the top competitors' brand evoke in the market? Are these working for them?

2. Firm's Differentiation

On what item or items will the firm differentiate itself on with respect to the competition and the potential customers? Will this generate a unique market position and/or barrier to others? Which one of these points of differentiation provides the best market position? Can your competitor claim this position or something close to it? If yes, re-examine the worksheets and identify a new point of differentiation.

What is the competitive strategy this point or points of differentiation support (e.g., price, feature/benefit, outcome, meaning, etc.)? How will this strategy be implemented within the firm?

3. Future History

Assume it is 20 years in the future and everything that the firm wanted to accomplish relative to the opportunity is complete. Write a brief entry in the encyclopedia (Wiki) of business about the firm from the vantage point of 20 years in the future. What does their success look like internally and externally? This relates to earlier worksheets. Consider what customers and other might be quoted as saying about the firm?

Worksheet 7 – Purpose

Finally the Purpose, Vision, and Mission Statements

Often companies start by formulating their purpose, vision, and mission statements before they do any other planning work. Of course, this isn't the process used here. Until the business environment is understood, the competitive strategy developed, an opportunity selected, the target customers known, and so on the firm isn't ready to work its purpose, vision, mission, and brand.

Established firms may state they already know their purpose, vision, and mission; therefore, they may want to skip ahead and forgo this work. That is their choice; however, it may be very illuminating to do those pages anyway. If they complete the worksheets they will either validate what exists or find out what may need repair or adjustment.

If the company is large and made up a number of business units their purpose, vision, and mission statements may become very high level and abstract. This occurs, because the firm is trying to make one statement cover all their operations. The higher the firm's level of diversification the vaguer and more abstract these statements become. This can often make converting the brand statement into behaviors difficult. One solution is to define the high-level cross-enterprise values, culture, etc. that all will follow, and then to create a more business unit specific set of brand behaviors that address a specific offering, local market or segment need.

First a Digression to Why, How, and What

Behind this worksheet and parts of others is an old strategy used to help develop the brand that Simon Sinek made popular in his book and talks called "Start with Why." Until he named it we didn't know it had a name. Congratulations, Simon! Okay, I am a little envious.

What is the highest level of differentiation that generally supports the best margins? It's meaning. People like to join with those that have similar beliefs, goals, and needs; therefore don't lead by selling the trinket, start by talking about what the firm believes and why it's in business. Connection through mutual beliefs helps create a spirit-to-spirit bond; in contrast to a trinket-to-wallet relationship.

- Why is the firm in business (purpose)?
- How does the firm achieve its purpose?
- What does the firm offer that expresses this uniqueness?

Purpose, Vision, and Mission

My process has specific meanings for purpose, vision, and mission that may not align with some organizations. I won't be so judgmental as to say I am right, but I highly suggest for these worksheets my definitions are followed.

Purpose is a simple direct statement of why the firm exists. Profit is not the reason. Profit is only a metric, or a measure. Perhaps the firm exists so a bunch of creative people can do fun stuff together, while making a living doing it. That's fine. Honestly is good. Maybe the firm's purpose is to give the world a healthy delicious alternative to candy, create safer water, or cut silicon wafer production's impact on the environment. Just keep it simple. If it goes into more than two sentences try again. The longer it is the less one has a clear idea. How will the business make life better on this planet?

The vision is a concise statement of what the world is like when the purpose is fulfilled. This is the new bliss created by the firm when it achieves its purpose. Every employee needs to understand and buy into the purpose and vision in order to achieve a healthy and optimal system.

Next are the major strategies, the broad statements on how the purpose will be achieved. These broad business strategies will later help generate departmental or functional business objectives which themselves will generate more specific strategies that drive the formation of major tactics.

The mission statement is often confused with the purpose statement. The mission is focused on the one pivotal strategy that must be done to attain the purpose. If the firm is a department store that is competing on lowest price then it may have a mission like, "Our mission is to squeeze every penny of cost out of our supply chain." Do you see a relationship between differentiation and mission?

Rallying Cries

The purpose can also serve as a rallying cry for the firm. Purposes that are rallying cries tend to be simpler, direct, and lower in the Maslow Hierarchy of Needs then more altruistic ones. The classic one is "Beat [competitor's name]," and this can work, especially when the firm's upper management is totally focused and dedicated to this task. However, there is a downside to this. What happens when the dog chasing the car finally catches it? What does the dog do now?

When the firm achieves the rallying cry it may experience a crisis, because what it has been doing may no longer be valid or the best approach going forward. Catching or over taking the market leader moves the firm from being the predator (the one chasing), to the prey (the one being chased). Firm's experiencing this change need to re-define their culture and brand with this process. Better is to anticipate over taking the leader and have a plan already polished and ready to implement when the underdog becomes the lead dog.

Quality, Great Customer Service, Lowest Price

What if the purpose is about having something like the highest quality, the best customer service, or the lowest price? These can be fine, but it is best to check to see if the item is a real purpose by asking, "What end is served by the firm's purpose being [item, like quality], or "Why is [item] important?" The answer to these questions can help determine whether it is a true purpose or a strategy to achieving a purpose.

A purpose that reflects the reason the firm exists (other than making money) from an honest and true position provides the best foundation for the brand.

Purpose Statement Examples

These purpose statements were taken from their websites. Some of these are labeled on their websites as purpose and others as mission statements. The difference between the two with respect to this workshop is mission statements expresses the key strategy. For example, Starbucks shows its strategy after the hyphen, while Burger King shows its starting with "…all freshly." Strategies in purpose or mission statements generally contain a hyphen, semicolon, or connecting words like by, in, and, with, through, and based on. It is best to keep purpose and mission statements separate for clarity.

Starbucks:

To inspire and nurture the human spirit – one person, one cup and one neighborhood at a time.

Burger King:

We proudly serve the best burgers in the business, plus a variety of real, authentic foods…all freshly prepared…just the way you want it.

The Boeing Company Vision:

People working together as a global enterprise for aerospace industry leadership.

Airbus Group:

Airbus Group aims for leadership of the commercial aeronautics and defense and space markets, based on its strong European heritage.

Microsoft:

Our mission is enable people and businesses throughout the world to realize their full potential by creating technology that transforms the way people work, play, and communicate.

Medtronic:

To contribute to human welfare by application of biomedical engineering in the research, design, manufacture, and sale of instruments or appliances that alleviate pain, restore health, and extend life.

Torie & Howard Candies:

We believe that food tastes better when it is made with organic, natural ingredients and responsible principles. We strive to create delicious, tasty treats that are made in a way that is as health-friendly, eco-friendly and socially conscious as possible.

BMW Automobile:

Sheer driving pleasure. Sporting and dynamic performance combined with superb design and exclusive quality.

As I stated before, when companies expand into different industries or contain a number of businesses their purpose, mission, and vision statements tend to become very generalized and similar to their competitors. A good example of this is the Airbus and Boeing statements above. In these cases, expressions of differentiation are often focused on a specific product or service brand.

Worksheet 7 – Purpose

1. Firm's Differentiation

From Worksheet 6.

2. Purpose

Other than making money or keeping customers happy, what is the reason the firm is in business? Refer to earlier worksheets. This should be no longer than one sentence, the more concise the better. Does the competitor have the same purpose? If yes, should the purpose be changed?

3. Vision

If the firm's purpose is fulfilled what will the future look like for those people and areas effected? This is a summary of the outcome from the "to be," state. Try to keep this concise and limited to five sentences. Does the firm still exist when the vision becomes reality? What will the firm be like once the vision occurs?

4. Strategies

What are the three to five key business strategies that will enable the firm to make the purpose and the vision come true? What are the specific marketing and communications strategies for positioning the firm and/or offerings?

5. Mission

Of the strategies listed in 7.4, which one is the key to achieving the purpose? Generally, there is one strategy that is pivotal to the success of the business. It is the strategy everything rest on. "Our mission is to do this [strategy....] in order to accomplish [big idea or purpose]."

6. Getting it Done

What are the two to five key things that describe how the firm turns its purpose into actions?

Worksheet 8 – Brand Architecture

A Promise Supported by Pillars

The brand has already been established as a series of behaviors expressed by the firm through its people, processes, and offerings. The previous material hinted that these behaviors spring from the company's purpose, values, competitive position, and differentiation. What organizes these behaviors into a cohesive set? The Brand Architecture is the framework that pulls it all together.

The Brand Architecture grabs the bits and pieces and glues them together into a coherent whole that eventually guides the development of the firm. The first piece is the brand promise. The promise is the purpose or the competitive differentiator rewritten as a commitment or outcome to the target customer segment. Walmart's slogan or tagline, "Save money, live better," is an expression of their brand promise.

How does Walmart save people money so they can live better? That's where the pillars come in. The pillars are the three to five items that enable Walmart to make good on their promise. We don't know what they use, but they could have something like highly managed supply chains, shared risk, avoid locating near big competitors, friendly service, and everything a family needs. Another company may have pillars like bold leadership, relentless relevant innovation, beautifully efficient, and trusted partner to support a promise like, "Breakthrough products that revolutionize the industry."

The pillars drive the structure, processes, and behaviors of the firm through the continual refrain of the question, "How can the organization fulfill this pillar? "

Not shown on the worksheet is an exercise I do after the brand pillars are established. We have the small teams go off and write one to two paragraphs that explain how each pillar supports the brand promise and expresses the firm's personality. Then each team shares their narrative for the first pillar, which is followed by a group discussion to help come to a common understanding. Then we do the second pillar using the same process and so forth. Notes are taken during the discussion.

After the workshop we take the narratives and notes and polish them; we create one short description for each pillar. This is not a process of working everyone's ideas in, but finding the most relevant supportive theme. These short explanations of the pillars will later become part of the architecture and more importantly part of the brand education process.

Linkage

This is obtained from an earlier worksheet. It is also a time to review and see if it is still valid or needs some refinement. What problem, need, conflict, or desire is the firm's brand going to be associated with? This helps inform the promotional strategy as well as business development.

Behavioral and Operational Attributes

Just as the pillars are the key to making the promise become true, the behavioral and operational attributes enable fulfilling the pillar. Another way of looking at this is the brand promise is the objective, the pillars are the strategies, and the attributes are the major tactics.

Originally I didn't draw a distinction between behaviors and operational attributes during a workshop. They were just lumped together. Now I try to do these as two separate exercises. But it can still be combined, but the separation occurs after the workshop.

First, assign a pillar to each individual team and ask them to brainstorm the attributes that create it. These are one to two word phrases. Have them list as many phrases as they can in five to ten minutes. To help get things started, provide a few examples of attributes that may go under a pillar. Don't forget attributes like fun, stylish, geeky, hip, tough, soft, or compassionate are acceptable and desired in addition to other dynamic and illustrative terms.

Then have the team select the top ten or twelve phrases that support the pillar, with emphasis of course on the most active, emotive, and dynamic attributes in the list. Next they return to the larger group to share and discuss their findings. After sharing the group selects the top five to eight attributes per pillar from all lists. Lastly, we have the group take five minutes to assign as many of the remaining terms to one of the top selected attributes. Some of these left over items may not fit with any of the chosen or selected attributes. All these attributes become part of the words-to-use list.

Follow the same process for the operational items, except don't limit the phrases to one or two words. Instead prompt for an actual name or very short description of the process or item. These lists are used extensively on worksheet 9.

Worksheet 8B

This is the easy worksheet. Worksheet 8A is transcribed to 8b using those small pieces of notepaper, usually yellow, with the tacky adhesive on the top of the backside, and containing only one item per note. [Note to firms, this is an ideal product placement opportunity – call now, reasonable rates.]

Why use the sticky notes? [Great place for a product name, call now.] I generally run an exercise where the group spends fifteen minutes ordering the behavioral and operational sections by importance to the pillar, brand, and mission. This will later guide the work with respect to time and budget during planning.

Worksheet 8A – Example

Below is an example for a B2B operation that may help illustrate this part of the process. The items in the example have been adjusted and the operational attributes omitted to protect the client. Notice that the attribute "practical" is coupled with this list of items on innovation. The behaviors surrounding "being practical" helps shift the focus from pure to applied research and development, informs the investment allocation to favor a mix that is more market driven than market driving, and reins in the wild west of "adventurous," with the assistance of disciplined processes.

Brand Pillar #1:   Relevant Innovation

Pillar Narrative: We are adventurous explorers determined to fulfill our need to create, invent, and commercialize revolutionizing technologies, methods, and practices that advance our industry, demonstrates our love and commitment for our customers, and periodically makes history.

Attributes

Determined	Targeted	Adventurous	Practical
• Persistent • Goal Oriented • Respectful • Engaged • Navigate • Confident • Negotiate • Assertive	• Industry - Customer Knowledge • Customer driven and customer driving • Accountable • Responsible • Responsive • User-centric	• Fearless • Seeker – Explorer • Experimenter • Imaginative • Finds a Way • Willing to Change • Limitless • Open	• Disciplined Processes • Consistent Rules • Achievable Goals • Synergies • Competitive • Learns • Balanced

The items not selected as one of the major attributes are assigned, if possible, to one of the chosen attributes. Not all attributes will find a home under one of the chosen ones.

The Pillar Narrative captures the spirit and intent with respect to the workforce. Writing from the workforce's point of view helps with education and implementation later. Below is another example of a pillar narrative. Imagine how that paragraph might impact the day-to-day operations of the firm. At least one of the pillars should address the key competitive differentiator.

One Community

We are a community of teams and individuals that together support each other in achieving our purpose and our need to learn and grow. Individually and within our teams we help to ensure the group's integrity and ethics. We honor each person simply for who they are and we understand that everyone is contributing the best they can at all times.

Worksheet 8A – Brand Architecture

1. Brand Promise

Restate the company's purpose or key point of differentiation as an outcome that is meaningful, relevant, and valuable to a customer.
How do you know this promise is meaningful, relevant, and valuable to customers?

2. Linked Problem

What customer desire or need is the brand going to be linked to? This informs the promotional strategy.

3. Brand Pillars

List three to five items (using one to three words) that identify what the firm needs to do to make the promise become true. These are like titles for categories or groups of activities. For example, relevant, innovation, young and fresh, or always organic. At least one pillar should be a key differentiator.

4. Behaviors

For each pillar list five to ten behavioral attributes that support the pillar. Use one to two words for each attribute. Attribute lists sometimes contain an item to check or balance the others, for example, if innovation is a pillar attributes may be awareness, exploration, creativity, and practical; where practical helps balance the other items.

An interesting exercise is to give people not involved in the workshop the list of attributes for a given pillar and then to ask them to find one or two words to summarize the grouping. Matching the actual pillar is nice, but not required. Gaining an understanding on the relationship between what the test group selected and the workshop group came up with can be very insightful.

5. Operational Attributes

For each pillar list five to ten operational attributes. These are the processes, methods, principles, structures or items that are key to enabling the success of each pillar. Often behaviors occur within or in support of these operational attributes.

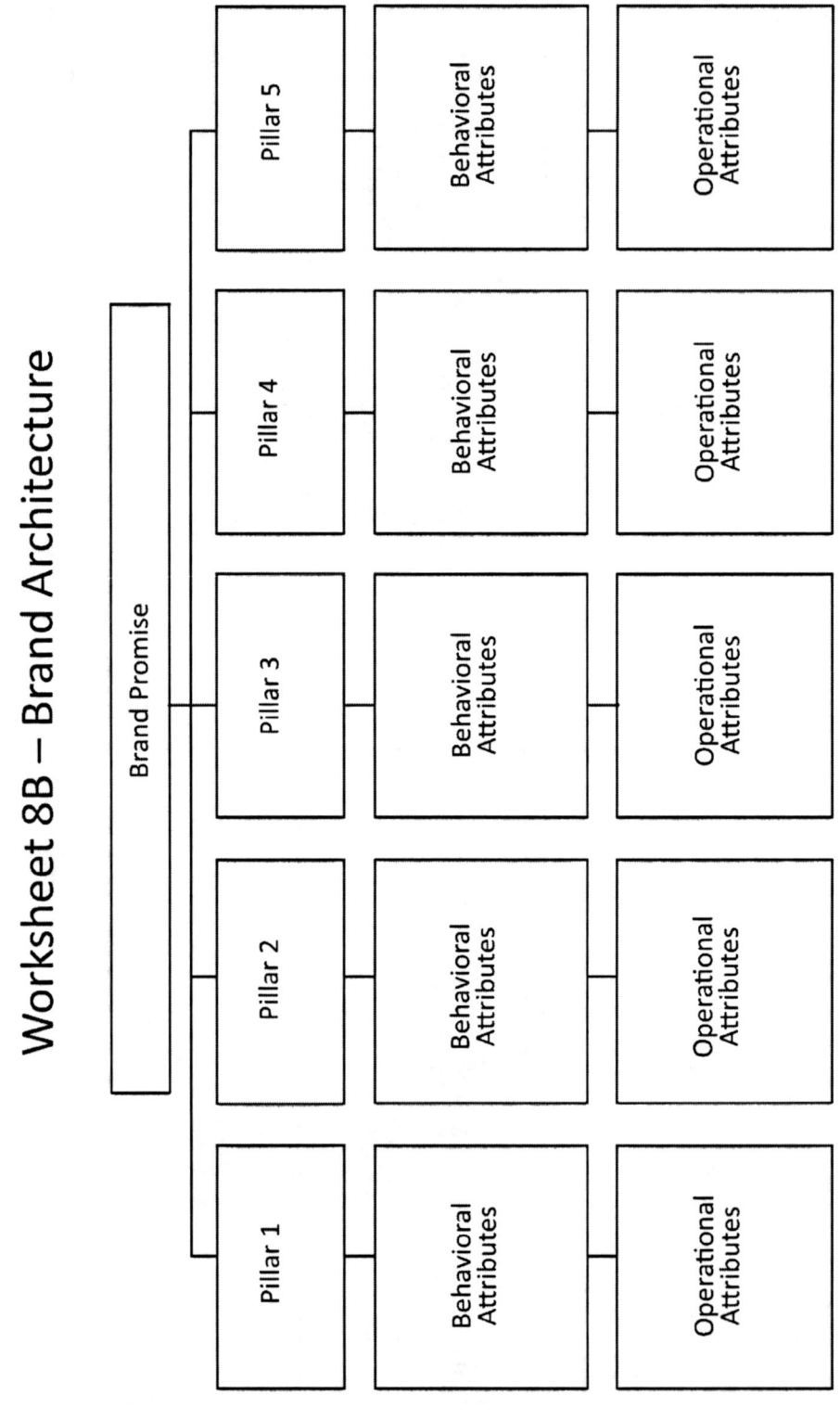

Worksheet 9 – Attribute Narratives

Now as the end of the workshop approaches everything is starting to fall in place. This next step transforms the brand strategy and architecture into the major tactics and actions that will make the brand real. The key to the narratives is asking, "How does the firm, department or team behave [attribute], or make it real?"

This worksheet seeds what will eventually become the product and service design principles and the organizational, behavioral, and operational tactics and processes that become the firm's culture. These narratives are inputs to a road mapping and planning workshop.

During the workshop have the small teams get started on building these narratives, but these are often finished in the polishing process. Narratives aren't always optimized when built by committee. Getting started on them in the workshop helps everyone get a firmer understanding on how to build the brand and provides the group a sense of ownership that will help later when bringing the brand to life.

Have the small teams take about 30 minutes to write a first draft of a narrative for a chosen attribute and its group. Due to the usual time limitations, assign one chosen attribute and its group to a team. If time permits, it's great to have teams do a second grouping, even if it overlaps another team's assignment. Comparing the differences between two or more teams doing the same attribute can be very revealing. I encourage limiting, or better, completely banning any corporate speak in the narratives. We want these to come from the heart and use active, emotional, and dynamic language.

Here are some questions to help get the small groups thinking:

- How can an organization be [insert attribute]?
- How do employees show they understand what [attribute] means?
- How can the level of [attribute] be measured?
- How does management support [attribute]?
- What is the up side of this [attribute] and how it is expressed?
- What is the downside and how will that be mitigated?
- What part of [will the customer experience?
- How is the [attribute] embedded in our offerings?

The other helpful tip for writing narratives is to give the small teams a point of view or "who's talking to whom" to help them frame their writing. The other important items are: 1) use as many or all the attributes assigned to the group in the narrative, and 2) if other attributes are needed go ahead and add them. A good narrative illuminates the business structure and the tactics that support it.

Below is an example of a write up for "Adventurous." Each narrative is written as if the brand is fully in place and successful. Each narrative is created without consideration to the other narratives. When all the narratives are completed they are read together against the brand structure and adjusted as needed. This example does not include the operational attributes.

Example - Adventurous

"We are fearless innovators who are ready to try new things, to change and evolve with the times, and are open and encouraging of imagination and new paradigms. Our culture balances the current mission needs with a commitment to give each other time to think, explore, express, create, and invent. We invest in learning and tools to support experimentation and development.

Our environment is open, collaborative, and strives to be limitless. We celebrate pushing the boundaries of "what is" regardless if we succeed or fail. Our motto, 'It is better to try and fail then not to have tried at all.'

Our organization is aware of the advancements going on outside our company and industry and we find ways to incorporate the best of these into our designs and processes. However, we are explorers, pioneers, and inventors first and farmers second."

Given the narrative above, is it possible to use those three paragraphs to help guide the development of the corporate culture, hiring process, and other business strategies and tactics? How would a manager lead, manage and hire given this attribute? If the entire firm was built around this one attribute would it be optimal? If yes, how would this create an optimal environment? If no, what other attribute, or attributes, are needed to achieve an optimal condition? Does this attribute support, "delivering breakthrough products that revolutionize the industry?"

The facilitator constructively challenges the group to ensure the narratives are supporting building a fully integrated brand.

Here are some helpful questions:

- What aspects of the narrative directly support the brand promise?
- Which items help other items support the promise?
- What items are needed, but don't impact the promise?

A Peak at Implementation

At this point in the process, the pillars and behavioral and operational narratives cover the overall direction of the enterprise. However, the enterprise-level behavioral and operational attributes and narratives may not be focused enough for individual departments to implement. During the implementation process individual departments and some key teams use the enterprise structure as a starting point to create their more specific list and narratives to act on.

This can feel a bit overwhelming for medium to large firms, but there are two ways to make this easier. Both methods start with educating management and the workforce on the business objectives, strategies, brand position, and architecture (including the existing narratives), and what their role is in making this structure real.

The first method is to have each department compose their own behavioral and operational attributes and narratives based on the firm's new brand pillars and the team's specific operational activities. This can take time and requires some mentorship from the cross-functional brand team. The advantage of this method is everyone is moving at the same pace together to get to strong vertically integrated organization. The second method focuses on building momentum for change through small victories in contrast to the first that prefers to have everything fully defined before change can begin.

The second method asks each manager and their team to learn and understand the pillars and the pillar narratives and then to identify one thing they can do within the next three-to-six months that is within their control to make the pillar real, or more real – stronger. As the team works on this focus item, the management team completes the first method. If the management team isn't done when the item is completed the team selects a second item to work on. Again, they rely on their own interpretation of the pillar narrative to select an action. Once the team members know the direction they usually will make good project selections.

Some departments, like finance, may not need to take the process very deep, but the rule of thumb here is the closer a group is to the customer (for example, sales, product development, or service) the more extensive and detailed will be the list of behavioral and operational attributes.

Worksheet 9 – Narratives

Pillar Number: Pillar Title:

Behavioral or Operational Attributes	Narrative
Behavioral Attribute #1	
Behavioral Attribute #2	
Behavioral Attribute #3	
Behavioral Attribute #N	
Operational Attribute #1	
Operational Attribute #2	
Operational Attribute #3	
Operational Attribute #N	

Duplicate this form as many times as needed to complete the narratives

Example: Documenting the Architecture

Worksheet 8B is a good form for providing an overview of the architecture. Below is an example of a format that can be used to document the details of the brand architecture. There are some place holders to help show the format and some chosen operational attributes and attribute groups were added as an example, but their narratives where not inserted. This format is followed for each pillar.

Brand Promise: We deliver breakthrough products that revolutionize the industry.

Brand Pillar #1: Relevant Innovation

Pillar #1 Narrative: We are adventurous explorers determined to fulfill our need to create, invent, and commercialize revolutionizing technologies, methods, and practices that advance our industry, demonstrates our love and commitment for our customers, and periodically make history.

Behavioral Attributes: Determined, Targeted, Adventurous, Practical

    Determined: Narrative here

    Targeted: Narrative here

    Adventurous: We are fearless innovators who are ready to try new things, to change and evolve with the times, and are open and encouraging of imagination and new paradigms. Our culture balances the current mission needs with a commitment to give each other time to think, explore, express, create, and invent. We invest in learning and tools to support experimentation and development.

    Our environment is open, collaborative, and strives to be limitless. We celebrate pushing the boundaries of "what is" regardless if we succeed or fail. Our motto, 'It is better to try and fail then not to have tried at all."

Practical:	Narrative here
Operational Attributes:	Disciplined Processes, Invest in People, Open and Loving, Principled Design
Disciplined Processes:	Narrative here (fair, consistent, meaningful, safe, efficient, nimble, agile, and compassionate)
Invest in People:	Narrative here (motivate, challenge, support, coach, reward, diversity, share, and reward)
Open and Loving:	Narrative here (communication, integrity, safety, empathy, compassion, and heart-to-heart)
Principled Design:	Narrative here (brand ambassador, standards, stylish, consistent, organic, user-centric)
Notes:	May include an explanation on how this relates to other pillars or other pillar attributes.

Worksheet 10 – Brand Personality

Going for the Bonus Level

Congratulations, at this point the brand architecture is roughed out and ready to send to polishing. The workshop attendees have qualified to go on to the bonus level. But first, check out if the participants are saturated, exhausted, or burned-out. If they are then it is alright to stop here, because the point of diminishing returns has been reached. However if they are up for it, here are two bonus worksheets.

The Brand Personality and Positioning Statement are part of two other workshops. Completing these sheets will provide a head start on the required follow-on work. The Brand Personality and Expression Workshop yields more detail and richness to the contents on this sheet to create the Brand Style Guide. The style guide documents how to communicate the brand via the senses: sight, sound, taste, touch, and smell as well as texture, tone, voice, emotion (feelings), and aesthetic.

If the firm or the offering doesn't have a name or logo, then the personality workshop results will help their development. Once the name and logo are determine the style guide includes the standards for their use as well.

The Positioning Statement is like a value proposition or elevator speech. This is a key document developed as part of the Integrated Marketing and Communications Plan Workshop. It isn't used outside of the firm; however, inside the firm it informs and guides the Marketing and Communications groups in developing their audience messages and marketing materials.

A Helpful Exercise

I like to start out without the worksheet and help them get into a more creative space with a white board exercise. Below are some of the questions I use in this exercise. This is a whole group activity where people get to shout out their responses. There are no wrong answers and there will be multiple answers per question. First, go through the questions asking for answers with respect to the firm now. Then ask, with respect to the firm after the new brand architecture is firmly established. I always use the first five questions the rest if there is time.

- If the firm was a celebrity who would it be?
- What television shows would it watch?
- What kind of car does it drive?
- What mythical creature, being, or item would the firm be?
- What foods does it like?
- What sports does it enjoy playing, if any?
- What animal represents the firm?
- What flavor of ice cream represents the firm?

- What color would it be?
- What sound would it enjoy?
- What does it feel like, texture?
- What shape represents the firm?
- A type of décor does the firm like?

After the answers are on the board, I do a vote to determine the top two or three responses to each question. I give everyone two to five votes to cast in each category. The number of votes provided depends on the length of the list. When completing the form the teams should think about how the top answers direct the firm's future Brand Personality. I use this same method to help inform the décor for the office, packaging, etc.

Here are two discussion questions that may be helpful:

- Is there a gap between the "as-is," or present personality, and the future "to-be" state?
- How will the gap be addressed?

Reversing the Process: Brand Personality to Opportunity Selection

Generally, I prefer to work in the order the worksheets are shown; however, as mentioned at the beginning of this guide, they can also be worked in reverse. It is possible to start with Worksheet 10 and work back up the process letting the personality guide the creation of the firm, offering, and strategies.

Below is an example of the steps that could be taken if the desire is to start with the personality.

1. Define what the future personality should be
2. Given step #1, determine the brand architecture that would be required to support it.
3. Look at all the pillars and attributes and determine what brand promise it yields up.
4. With the brand promise determined construct the purpose, mission, vision, etc. that aligns with it.
5. Identify the customer type that the firm would love having a long-term relationship with.
6. Determine what offerings the firm could develop that would create the most enjoyment and love between the company and the customer base.
7. Examine the business environment that the firm-customer relationship will exist in and see how this affects the work already done in the previous steps. Refine as needed.
8. Do the SWOT Analysis and select the offering that provides the best competitive advantage.

Some steps omitted for brevity.

Worksheet 10 – Brand Personality

1. Brand Personality

Draw on the earlier worksheets to help in completing this one. Concisely describe the firm's personality using active, emotional, dynamic, and illustrative language. It should be congruent with the promise, pillars, and attributes. It may help to think of the firm as a person entering and participating at a party. Although this was covered earlier, it is a good time to refine it now that architecture and narratives are completed.

2. Colors

What colors and tones express the brand? What are these colors expected to represent or evoke?

3. Sounds

What sound or music style expresses the brand? What should the sound evoke in a listener? Feel free to list a few songs as examples.

4. Textures

What textures express the brand and what are these expected to evoke? It may help to describe how they feel against the fingers, face, etc.

5. Shapes

What shapes express the brand and what are these expected to evoke?

6. Other

Classic, traditional, contemporary, modern?

Energy level?

Traditionalist or futurist?

Regional, local, or international?

Warm or cold?

Worksheet 11 – Positioning Statement

The Positioning Statement is a key document used to help guide the development of the Integrated Marketing and Communications Plan. It isn't generally used outside of the firm, but it guides the creation of external messages, the elevator speech, and value proposition. Below is the format I use.

Structure:

For the customer:	Name of segment
Customers' desire?	What the customer wants to achieve.
Firm's Name:	Name
Unique thing the firm does for the customer's desire:	[Name of the key unique differentiator] enables the [name of potential customer segment] to achieve [the desire or outcome and possible measure].
How it does it:	Describe briefly the pivotal way, or ways, the unique thing delivers value. This may also include other differentiators or patents.
Reason to believe the claim:	Compelling evidence that give your potential customer confidence in the firm and its offering – proof points.
Close:	Very short restatement of value to the market

Positioning Statement Example

"For integrated circuit manufactures committed to decreasing their environmental impact, WidgetWiz Inc. provides WaferForge with ResouceSaver technology. WaferForge is the industry's newest high-capacity small footprint refining system for silicon wafer production. The WaferForge has the highest-capacity of any forge in its class, and its patented ResourceSaver protocols save 25% in energy and 10% in water per wafer over previous models. Gains like this are achieved from our patented three-way ultrasound zone refining system and our water management algorithms and feed-forward predictive protocols. Manufactures who are using WaferForge have significantly decreased their environmental impact while increasing production." – 96 words

Since I work mostly in the B2B world this example has worked well for me. I also use this example as part of an exercise to teach how to rewrite one with more emotional, active, and dynamic language. This one needs the rewrite.

After introducing the position statement format, I share the example statement with the group. Then in the large group, I asked them to match the phrases or sentences in the example to the individual parts of the format. It is highly recommend that facilitators write their own example centered in the types of businesses they typically support.

Strategic Positioning Test

The positioning statement directs the marketing and communications groups in their promotional planning. The firm's strategic market position should be clearly articulated in the statement. In the WidgetWiz example, the firm is positioned primarily as the environmental leader to those customers who hold environment as important.

Have the small groups each draft a positioning statement, report to the larger group, and then spend time discussing and hopefully arriving at a strong and concise statement.

If I feel the group has trouble creating concise materials then I will either be more directive during the group discussion and group rewrite, or tell them they are limited to 75 or 100 words. For value propositions and product definitions, I will generally place the limit at 35 or 50 words. A fully understood idea can be communicated succinctly.

Next, have the group list the top three competitors to the firm and/or the offering and the top three alternative competitors, if any. An alternative competitor is an indirect competitor to the entire market segment. For example, airlines directly compete with each other, but indirectly with video conferencing - the alternate competitor.

Then have the group list next to each competitor what they believe or know is each company's position with respect to the target customer segment. Ask participants to examine the listing and discuss what it may mean to their firm's position. The final positioning statement will come out of the polishing process.

Worksheet 11 – Positioning Statement

Inputs for the Positioning Statement

Name of target customer segment	
Customer's desire or need	
Firm's name	
Name of key unique diffentiator that enables the customer to achieve their aspiration	
Describe briefly the pivotal way, ways, the firm delivers value to the customer	
Proof points - evidence the gives the potential customer confidence in obtaining the promised value	
Close - short re-statement of value to the market	

Create the Positioning Statement:

Another Sneak Peak at What's Next

What happens next is to determine how each group will behave or implement the pillars and/or key attributes. Specifically, how employees will live the brand within the context of their tasks and interactions within the firm and with customers. Our starting point begins by developing customer experience maps. Then we use the maps to determine where the key brand moments will be along the journey. Armed with the list of brand moments a firm then provides the training, resources, and design principles to empower these moments. This is how a firm vertically integrates its brand into the customer experience.

Below is a small slice from one of our types of experience maps. This example begins when the customer first thinks about the need for the offering and then continues by identifying each step along their journey from procurement, through use, and then into retirement of the offering. At each step, we look to see what is happening between the firm and the customer in order to identify ways to express the brand uniquely and meaningfully. In addition to this map, we use event mapping to detail out the key brand moments and identify how to deliver them.

The process for this table starts with completing the lower three rows for each column and then working through the pillars one column at a time. Identify potential brand moments that resonant with the customer and firm with respect to the pillar. Not every step will have a brand moment. Remember pillars carry attributes with them.

Pillar	Customer thinks about a warm beverage while out driving	Sees "The Teahouse"	Parks and enters the building
Pillar 1			
Pillar 2			
Pillar 3			
Pillar 4			
What does the customer want or need?			
What does the firm want or need?			
What is/are the brand moment, or moments?			

Using the Worksheets

Use of the Worksheets

Before getting into the dos and don'ts I want to make it clear I do want people to use the worksheets; however, don't abuse the copyright. The workbooks for the attendees are very inexpensive.

The buyer of the workbook and guide may use these materials within their own company or internal operations to help plan a start-up or for their own education and exploration. In these cases, the worksheets are free to use and copy. A request via www.heartcentricmarketing.com enables the owner of this guide to receive a pdf and Microsoft PowerPoint version of the worksheets via email.

What someone can't do is use any of these worksheets in any service or product offering, whether for a fee or free, outside of the use describe above. We are happy if you do want to incorporate them into your offerings, but we want you to pay a reasonable licensing fee. This includes educational institutions. I leave it to your own honor and integrity to police this request. Licensing is very affordable.

Contact Information

Feel free to email me questions on this material and/or provide feedback.

David A. Okrent
Okrent Consulting Services
Telephone: + 1 206 390-3806
Email: info@okrentconsultingservices.com
www.okrentconsultingservices.com
www.heartcentricmarketing.com

Check out Okrent Consulting Services on Facebook.

CPSIA information can be obtained
at www.ICGtesting.com
Printed in the USA
LVOW09s1910160817
545249LV00016B/109/P

9 780692 514290